chamber after chamber

chamber after chamber

SAARA MYRENE RAAPPANA

UNIVERSITY OF MASSACHUSETTS PRESS
Amherst and Boston

Copyright © 2024 by University of Massachusetts Press
All rights reserved
Printed in the United States of America

ISBN 978-1-62534-778-7 (paper)

Designed by Sally Nichols
Set in Adobe Jenson Pro
Printed and bound by Books International, Inc.

Cover design by adam b. bohannon
Cover art by painting cat, *untitled*, 2023. Courtesy of the artist.

Library of Congress Cataloging-in-Publication Data

Names: Raappana, Saara Myrene, author.
Title: Chamber after chamber / Saara Myrene Raappana.
Description: Amherst : University of Massachusetts Press, 2024. | Series:
   Juniper Prize for Poetry |
Identifiers: LCCN 2023046524 (print) | LCCN 2023046525 (ebook) | ISBN
   9781625347787 (paperback) | ISBN 9781685750725 (ebook)
Subjects: LCGFT: Poetry.
Classification: LCC PS3618.A3227 C47 2024 (print) | LCC PS3618.A3227
   (ebook) | DDC 811/.6—dc23/eng/20231017
LC record available at https://lccn.loc.gov/2023046524
LC ebook record available at https://lccn.loc.gov/2023046525

British Library Cataloguing-in-Publication Data
A catalog record for this book is available from the British Library.

CONTENTS

CONTENTS

He means to tell people about the light
but each part of his body revolts . . .

It wears pitch black shadowless silk
like a government official donning a tailored uniform

Yet he still speaks of light—and for light
he daily lowers himself underground
    —DU YA, *The Coal Miner,*" translated by Anni Liu

There is a vast melancholy in the canticles of the wolves,
melancholy infinite as the forest, endless as those long
nights of winter and yet that ghastly sadness, that mourn-
ing for their own, irredeemable appetites, can never move
the heart. . . .
    —ANGELA CARTER, *The Bloody Chamber*

chamber after chamber

WHEN I SAY *HEART*

I mean that once upon a time   Lionhearted Richard fell   arm arrow-

struck and gangrenous   his wartime kin embalmed his heart

with quicklime   frankincense   and spice

they locked it in a leaded box to keep starved wolves

from tracking and devouring it   they mixed and cast

what spells they had to render Richard's many-chambered life

into the stillest   flattest stone

HEART OF LION, HEART OF LIGHT

Kelly and I are making valentines from Mom's old books. One says a wild lion's heart
weighs twelve hundred grams, a man's heart just over three hundred;

and that, in 1901, to circumvent the soul's unseeability, doctors weighed six patients who,
in dying, lightened some: twenty-one recorded grams per immortal soul.

(Those same doctors—pioneers
—weighed dying dogs and certified, they said, the soullessness of beasts.)

But when Kel reads aloud—*i carry your heart with me (i carry it in my heart)*—we
    don't assume
that Cummings boxed his lover's chambered organ up inside his own.
So *heart* can't be mere muscle, and four lions' souls can fit inside a single human heart.

When dying Richard I the Lionheart (arrow, gangrene, opaque heat) forgave
the Châlus boy who'd shot him dead, Richard gripped that child's fist
and whispered, *by my bounty know the light of day.*

Richard's cooks knew meat, how best to keep it; they embalmed
his heart and put it in an iron case for transport home to Normandy.

(Envision a soul as light. See four chambers of light rising.)

When today's archaeologists sieve the dust of Richard's heart,
they find daisies, mercury, and frankincense. Plus creosote and lime (perhaps).
    Britannica
calls it *unsightly*: something that's impossible to see.

Kelly and I swoon over the Châlus boy (minutes before he realized the men approach-
    ing meant
to butcher him for butchering the Lionheart) walking through the cornered streets
the way light saunters over wild clematis. Picture that boy

like Richard and his lion's heart advancing on the Holy Land: breastplate barrel-wide,
ribs straining with heart. Imagine pioneers who theorize
but never see the light inside him lioning.

ONCE UPON AMERICA

My cousin Kelly returns from summers in Detroit. We play alien invasion and
    lost at sea,
drape sheets on chairs, the couch, and crouch inside. We hide from wild things.

I want to play Terminator war, LA 2025, the fight to save humanity,
but Kel thinks forests dark with life advance on us with beasts and witchery.

Outside (the real outside) irrigation crooks the black spruce twigs, drowns moss.
It muddies what short path fixes our house to wilderness.

Kel says *it's cats and dogs out there*. We picture them:
Lions bite our sheets, and she-wolves roar, read bones that say a forest life

will tenderize and mull our hearts into good spell ingredients.
We invent stars to count to quell imagined panic: three stars

of Batman's hi-tech belt, and Millennium Falcon Major, Millennium Falcon Minor.
I drift off to sleep while Kelly spins a tale of two kids

lost walking in a forest with a basket of apocalypse. They come upon a witch's den.
They claim she tries to eat them, but their guns and germ-laced coverlets are too
    much war for her.

They name her home after themselves and teach her how to read.
They whip her if she fails to call out to their gods to cure her pain.

SPAWNING SEASON

I use scissors to behead them, then the dull
back of a *puukko* blade to flake the floor
with what, in death, are shiniest. My bullshit
childhood chore: to find and tug the slimy cord
of life—spleen, air bladder, and from the perch's
throat, the heart's soft nugget. I was raised
by women who could gut any fish, who
told me males were quick. But females, bellies
blister-pale, would spill complications.
My mother combs roe from my hair
and says, *flood. I feel a flood coming.*

WHEN I SAY *HEART*

I mean that in tenth grade   when Mr. Barry ordered bovine hearts

for Bio-1 dissection   they arrived sliced

open   unrolled flat

because he hadn't checked the box that specified

he wanted hearts to study   not to eat

that's how I learned

the heart   pressed flat   is meat

FLOOD COMING

In the aquarium's ocean corridor,
I hug a notebook to my chest. Jason
Holmson backs me toward the corner,
describing cuttlefish. I ache for him
like hell and so I let him tell me what I know already:
that to mate, cuttles go red; in frigid alcoves,
black. That their venom can steal anybody's breath.
But Jason's eyes like casting spoons, his thumbs that probe
the dimple of my back and tug me up:
The flush of air, exposure, so I run. Tonight, in bed,
I'll spin and spin, heart a hook in my throat.

SELFIE AS ELLY THE DOLL

I hear things. Like, that burnout who held another
by the river, by the neck? He didn't love her.

He told Feck he stopped her breath to stop her talking
shit; it made him feel alive. I've never been.

To seem like other girls, I wear a dress.
and when Feck (that's my fella) lifts

me up, I dance. My bones are air; my lips
designed to whistle how a nice girl won't. The skinned

fish of my tongue can't feel his kiss, and that,
I think, is best. When Feck (he's crying) casts

my body to the river, I'm grateful for the chance
to rest and travel. Wind tickles my feet until I dance,

and currents lift me even higher than
I got when Feck and I first met:

he gripped my neck and took
my nozzle in his teeth, exhaling hard. I shook

as wishes filled me up; I almost popped, and Feck
looked almost human then. He kissed my head

while my eyes wept (what love, what tenderness)
a sky of sinsemilla clouds across the bed.

SMOKE

As in:
You can tell the source by its color

If eye-white   Noxzema   cotton swab
then moisture   or   a freshly burning thing

and if soup spoon   gypsum   raincloud   key
then Frisbee   Barbie   Matchbox car

and if lake ice   wrist veins   Zoloft   sky
then Marlboro   pipe   or steamroller

but if crude oil   midnight   fry-pan   tire
then black fire   steel char   blindrun   gone

As in:
What we steal from Kelly's father
and from our handsy, stingy boyfriends,
we take behind the sauna. We pick, pack, giggle, hiss.
I hide what's left inside my Care Bear's head
so later I can light the snow-soaked tree
that bares its boughs inside me.

As in:
My mother at the sink   ash-sizzle in the whiskey glass
My mother and the curtains drawn   her dark and spinning room

My father   midnight   on the porch alone
his orange-red cherry   visible to everyone

As in:
What seeps in or what escapes.
What I blow into a stuffed toilet paper tube,
go tiptoe to release. What seeps ventwise
to the visitation room to stroke
my mother's wrist, her ash-dry hair.

As in:
What tells me wind-direction
how quick   how mad

What tells me —stop— before I turn the knob

What tells me —sure   walk through that door
but only if you want to inhale fire—

WINTER CORRESPONDENCE

Demeter to Persephone / My mother to me

You pulled that man up like a root—snake-limbed, sulfuric, old
—and followed him down south, foolish as a thresher tilling snow.

I wrist-tested sunlight, microwaved Lake Superior in a bowl.
Still, your toes grew icicles. He offered rugs that melted snow.

You write, call me a chainsaw. True, when I try to coo, I growl.
But saplings don't run when groves rumble. They sprinkle leaves like snow.

Winter's my new daughter. In our kitchen, sleet blows.
No lust can smolder hot enough to soften her bricks of snow.

I soak cod in birch-ash, won't eat. I toss lutefisk to crows
and shiver. I cough up blizzards, spreading viruses of snow.

I do jumping jacks lying down: It's my second go at molding
angels. Both times, dear girl, I've failed. I've just built walls of snow.

For you, I'd drive as far as I could go, tire chains groaning road
to road, but I fear your trail's gone cold. It died in drifts of snow.

Persephone to Demeter / Me to my mother

Your e-mail says you've chilled the tussock sedge, taught it not to grow,
that the bowsaw of you, Mother, carves angels from hard-packed snow.

You grew me like your pear tree: boughs split, espaliered in rows
like candelabras. My elbows shook in sleeves as crisp as snow.

Crowned in sweat and DEET, I herd mothers' souls. They pluck "loves me / not"
from asphodel. Dunes of lonely petals shroud my feet like snow.

They say your new child's frigid, throws fits—flops to the ground and groans
no matter how your twilight skirts *shush* across her cheeks of snow.

I wish I'd met my winter sister. We'd make forts of pillows
and fjords. But if I'm home, she'll vanish like dimes dropped in snow.

You say my love's a combine that tries to throttle grain from snow.
It's true: though wheat frosts over, love works that field down to its bones.

I dial your number, Mama. I tap Morse Code into the phone.
There's only static. Your lines are down. They died in drifts of snow.

SUPERMAN AND BATMAN SLEEPOVER

A roof. Night sky. We make ourselves stories:
Kelly's homeworld lost to fire, escape pod
streaking past the stars, a crash.
For me, the stars are unstrung pearls
that ping through asphalt sky.
Moon turns her face to see me,
then she dies. Something dark inside me puts on wings.
Kel says that both our nighttimes
are the same: sky calling us to join its black expanse.
Her hair billows its long red cape. She inches toward the edge.
She says that Kryptonite's a rock floating through space
until it lands on Earth and turns into a hunk of neon gravity.
I grip her arm in one hand and the chimney in the other.
If we pretend enough,
will razors buckle
when Kel tries to cut her wrist? I mean
I wish invincibility on both of us:
Skin as clean as space or wealth, strong limbs
that aren't beholden to the ground.
But *invincible* isn't a word we get
to choose, except
in those few moments
when a fall
still feels
the same
as flight.

LITTLE RED AND LITTLE RED

Once upon a time   a lake   deadfall as couch

a twitch-eyed rabbit   and her rapid   pear-seed heart

Kelly and me listening   lanternless and pipe-lit

in a Have-You-Seen-Me?-poster-tinted   wilderness

where   we imagine   woodsmen   dressed like murderers

are hiding   drooling for our teen-sweet flesh

each time   a dry spruce needle snaps   we flinch

and laugh but then   applebait crunch   the stringtrap cracks

we wire-hang feet   unzip the fur and pull it back

to hood the rabbit head   then stick   fire

and sweating meat and upthroat   tonguecurl   wolfhowl teeth

at night   at home   I dream a woodsman

spicing grandma meat   with ash from shopping malls

I wake   and drive to town   so Kel and I can smoke a bowl

and giggle   like two girls chewing safe burgers   in a starlit parking lot

where all the hunters idling to wait   have dribbled motor oil

we lean against the hood   the constellations   high   regarding us

I think that I hear   Lupus growl   and cool my cheek

against the car   while Kel   who's fallen   roars her laugh

louder than chopping wood   and looking at   my face reflected

in the rainbow oil   says   *what a giant   pretty smile you have*

WHEN I SAY *HEART*

I mean   that mammals grow   four rooms

with walls that close   to press oxygen through

we carved our names

what keeps dead stand from turning into deadfall is the root

that burrowed deep   resists the squall   beetles   and rot

in wintertime Kelly and I would run into the woods with coats unzipped

to shake birch trunks and glut our throats on kifed communion wine

then   heavy-lidded   fall and press rough angels of ourselves into the snow

sometimes we ripped hand-me-down tees apart and braided them

we tied those bracelets to our bloodied wrists like sisterhood

we carved our names on trees that   dead   still stood

and wore our blood-wine teeth like dresses tight as bark

Kelly planted her feet in lake and said

that red is hearts and lips and cherry gum

and if you look like something begging to be chewed

no one will see how deeply into hell you've grown

the news says *rural epidemic*   but I don't feel feverish

I feel like birchbark peeled away no matter where I live

each time I asked about the scars that seamed my mother's wrists

she lied and said she'd toppled from a tree onto a nail in middle school

the part where gravity needs blood to let you fly is true enough

I'll fly to Sichuan years from now   but my dreams will still be lake

will still be home   where I'm a driftwood log   awash

and squinting through Superior's skin into the undertow

at Mother and our grandma and our aunts   at their wounds rendered

near-immodest by the deep lake's lapping   and Kelly's under water

laughing   ankles braceleted with black rock

she's implanted in the lakebed

branches of her hair outspread but

I'm unrooted.

Kelly I'm sorry

I can't stop floating away

II

ALL I KNOW OF WHITE

I learned from my mother when she dyed
my communion dress green.
Her thimbled, spit-wash thumb, her tisk.
White shows every spot, she said.
At home, my dad says, *Kissa died* and then
keeps on—shrinks from the weed eater's touch;
sings the hymns of put-off projects. August
is a skunk-hot lake. I hold my breath,
let horseflies bite. Above the bone grin
of his clerical collar, Dad's face lobsters
in the heat, runs sweat tributaries down
the La-Z-Boy wagon-print plush.
Shoeboxed, dirt-brindled, that old white cat
goes rot-humid all day in the parched clematis.
I trowel the hole alone. I watch shadows
close on her like arms crossing to hide
a missing button, a patch of blemished skin.

WHEN I SAY *HEART* I MEAN

that to dissect the organs Mr. Barry handed out

Kelly and I ticked back and forth

between the cow's limp heart and bio textbook diagrams

we had convinced ourselves that we were wise

enough to take a thing our world had crushed and sold

and planned to eat and   like two awful

Jordached gods   restore it to its shape

PARADISE BY THE PAULDING LIGHT

We're too busy mining to be scared.
          —*IfIHadAHifi*

When Kelly flipped her Jeep (roll bar crushed straight
and seatbelt split), they said she'd never wake.

When she sat up, they said she'd never speak.
They claimed her wrapped eyes wouldn't see,

but when they rolled the bandage off, she saw.
We drove—she drove us—out past Watersmeet.

At midnight, there, they say ghost lights emerge:
A train, iron miners: spectral, lanterned,

searching. They say the lights start slow,
speed up, revolve; they almost burn your skin.

Stay still, though; they'll dissolve. We're waiting,
still. I ask her what she met the night

she crashed full-body into death. Half-past
midnight: Silence. No lights. Nothing.

Kel laughs and turns away and spits and says, *fuck this.*
But does she mean the mine that died,

the stitches in her head, the iron-hard sky
—maybe whatever flies as if to knock you dead

but brushes lightly past your cheek instead.

HOME PERM

Within the bonnet dryer's tonic of heat
       my grandma steeps   as if she's not

the bait-strung string   of Dilaudid evenings
       she stops filing DNRs

coughing red blooms   and growing roses
       out of ruin   she unfolds

in a blush of cheek   in a headstrong calm
       more buoyant than disease

teased out   how artfully she blinks
       and darts her eyes   as if the mirror

were the threshold   of lake crowded
       with surprise   then rises

uncoiling   the way a line   clipped
       by a fish-tooth   springs

CANTICLE OF WAITRESSES, WAITING

November 29, 2010, Marinette, Wisconsin

This is how we herd by the waitress station
while snow settles
like a nightgown, smothering what ails us.

How we first hear about the hostages
on Facebook, and then the whole town kneels,
still as snow once it resolves itself to ground.

How the sidewalk still needs seeding with rock salt.
How even when a person stands still, they can slip.

How we count the seeds of our blessings.
How our blessings rebound off the booths like buckshot.

How we each sometimes rebound into being
a country of one self.
How we other times are one self of a city.

How only below zero can we remember
September as that country where we save daylight
like fat over our muscles.

How a woman runs at the chained gym doors
to save her daughter.
How she drops on the unseeded walk.
How we'll remember her legs as
a fleet of hummingbirds skidding through snow.

How sometimes, to give something a shot means kill it.
How other times, it means close your eyes.

A MOTH

For two days, she, drenched
    in sunlight's endless,
        miniscule amendments,

rimpled
    like threadbare, piebald
        folds of mesh sifting

through a rice field or
    the Everglades.
        I've no clue why I

stepped on her and then
    assumed she'd died when,
        instead, she'd moored herself

within a guise of death,
    as if inside some
        couture dress, hand-sewn

so arabesquely
    you forget there's
        any woman in it.

So, couchside, I chew
    mooncakes, downloading apps
        for keeping track of *Idol*,

perps who confessed on
    SVU, and actions
        you can't go back on,

such as when, above
    the lake, you dangled
        your cousin's army doll,

and, blinking, let go.
    When one antennae,
        then one leg flitter

in no millimeter's
    worth of wind, my conscience
        churns like current

damned by narcissistic
    ballast, or maybe just
        by chance, to wash,

day after minnowed
    day, the naked
        face of evidence.

WHEN I SAY *HEART* I MEAN

a chunk of body breathing blood

a fragile   chambered organ that condemns

the brain to rot if it allows itself to sleep   tired flesh

inside tired flesh that   like a fist   has to unfurl

to keep from choking what it wants to hold

AFTER THE FUNERAL, AUNT SALLY TELLS A STORY WE'VE NEVER HEARD BEFORE

She says the sheets, hung out, shook like hung sheets
and that the gun, set out, lay quiet as a gun.
My grandpa drank a gin fifth in the heat.
And Sally, just turned ten, hummed every single song

she knew. A sheet exists to fold and fold
again, a wife to fold her children to herself,
and gin to fold a man until he's no
real man. My grandpa slid his pistol off the shelf

and tipped its open mouth against my granny's mouth.
Her lips, pressed tight together, looked as red
and heavy as a movie kiss. When Gramps finally passed out,
Sal prayed the sheets would shield them while they fled.

The smoke Aunt Sally smokes today is closing on the bone,
and larks, like larks, call out a song that fans
like something clean and light across Gran's marker stone.
Not one of us will speak of this again.

THE WOLF IN THE TRAILER,

tired of drinking every meal, licked the last bowl
till it was dry and fled into the darkened woods
because she couldn't stand it here
(lamplight like snakes biting her eyes)
but soon returned because forest at daybreak fills
itself with such undimmability.
Panting with the kind of pain that makes
people forget which lie they told themselves,
she moves from chair to chair as if a ray
were chasing her (her feet crack scattered dishes like
they're chipmunk bones). The paramedics, when
they force the door, will find her curled as if
in sideways prayer, head resting in a spot
of dawn so clear that they'll mistake her fur
for hair. One man will crouch and touch two fingertips
below her ear to prove no sun beats there.

TORCH

I've heard that in Cappadocia,
        where they say light
                cools malaria
        and draws husbands to
the ugly, women
        string trees with evil-eye
                amulets: catch dawn
        with the hollows
of blue irises.
        Light, we say, is hope:
                candle, ambulance,
        every torch carried.
So the blank aperture
        of a rice-sized camera
                swells to rule out cancer,
        and each zebra-pupil
on the twilit caldera
        expands as zebras
                rest in tandem
        —chin-on-shoulder,
and chin-on-shoulder
        —in case enough hope,
                collected, repels lions.
        When Kelly's ex texted
to say he'd like
        to shoot her, the cops said
                all you can do is
        watch, watch everything.

Her bedroom is unlit
        candles, hemp cloth
                kerosene-heavy
        in its sconces,
the whole earth black, and
        I lie wide-eyed until
                hope, rising, shrinks
        the hollow of the world.

CONFESSION OF THE LESSEE

Landlord, forgive the door screen that I split
stumbling with firewood in my arms,
a childhood rite that doesn't translate
to this brownstone's forced-air heat.
O you who burns the wind to keep
me warm, I also tore the rug
you left beside the hearth.
My feet are forest monsters wearing boots.
I wish that I could glide the way
my neighbor does: upon stilettoed shoes
that keep her slender heels at least
three inches off a ground that's paved
with manmade stone designed to keep
SUV tires from touching dirt.
We're both estranged by brick, linoleum,
or shoes. The word, I think, is *rent*.
Why do I feel so lost for leaving land
I've always wanted to disown? Landlord,
I keep exhaling bellows on this kindling,
but these flames refuse to weave
unless it's how Algoma iron, in subsoil,
finds another home:
too slow for any mortal to perceive.

WHEN I SAY *HEART* I MEAN

that once I read in *Time* about a girl who
      walking home from school   picked up a round

and stone-ish thing   but since she was in U.S.-occupied Iraq
      no heart-shaped thing wasn't a bomb

a doctor pulled bundles of blood-embroidered gauze
      out of her gasping chest   and called her Lion Heart

MY BRUSH

— Chengdu, Sichuan

I tap on Tang Laoshi's bedroom door and say *duibuqi,*
duibuqi, wo cui ni de jia.

(*Sorry, sorry, I break your home.*) I'm embarrassed
at what few words I know to tell her

I've dropped my brush and it's disappeared
into the shower drain—which is also a squat toilet

—and I'm worried. Moving to Sichuan to teach English, I followed
packing lists I found on the Internet. I packed too many

bottles of shampoo. Two hundred pairs of earplugs. Thick wool socks
for August. I am living with Tang Laoshi and her son

and his wife and their daughter to be immersed
in China's common language. To practice

drinking radish soup with dinner. I am learning to leave
some rice in the bowl to show that I'm thankful to be given

more than I need. At dinner, Tang Laoshi turns the lazy Susan
until the dish of rabbit is, to me, invisible. She says, *we know*

Americans don't like to see the face of what you eat.
I try again to explain that I dropped my brush

into the drain where we pee and shit and wash away
leftover rice. I am afraid my stupid Walgreens brush

will clog up the building. I am thinking of the time, as a kid,
I dropped a GoBot in the toilet, and we had to use only

our wood-and-nails-and-newspaper outhouse
for a week, and my mom hated walking to the treeline

in the dark, and my cousins from downstate laughed
and Kelly said I was a bear that shit in a hole in the ground.

But the hole where my brush disappeared is porcelain,
attached to a pipe that's attached to every apartment

in the building. I'm the foreigner
who won't look the rabbit I am eating in the face.

And now Tang Laoshi is telling me, *sorry, sorry*
let's get your brush, and something in Chinese I can't

understand and I'm saying, *duibuqi, duibuqi, wo cui ni de jia*,
and we are both so sorry. We work with a coat hanger

and string, we thread a magnet, then a fishhook,
and she is talking, and I don't understand, and we keep at it.

A year from now, I'll have learned to speak more Mandarin.
After climbing five flights of stairs to my own apartment

in another province, I will wash leftover rice into the hole
in my bathroom floor and, as the rice races down, down

through the building, I'll remember the words Tang Laoshi
said over that toilet and realize she was just sad for me

because a woman needs her brush.

PSALM WITH PLEATHER TEDDY BEARS

—Anshun, Guizhou

At first, I notice not Jing Jing at her soup stall but her shoes: Purple. Toes tipped
with pleather teddy bears. She lifts her ladle full of hog-skin curls in hen-foot broth.
She points and says my hair is yellow as the sunshine in America.

She says, *Transformers, Madonna, Beyoncé, Titanic.* She says American girls are all
in love with love. American girls are all in sex with sex.
She taps her muddy gym-shoe bears. We both laugh a bit hysterically.

In Florida, once, this crypto-hobo hipster took me dumpstering, and, sorting
    rotten fruit
from good, told a parable that, *down there*, all women are the same
shade of America. I laughed again. I laughed *politely*. I feel terrible enough

to reach into the earth, straight to America, and pull him through.

Today, my mom Skyped in to say that Kelly died: a razor blade, risperidone.
As kids, we'd play Columbus. She'd stand up tall—naked,
wearing bubbles—and yell, *THIS BATHTUB IS AMERICA.*

Jing Jing hands her baby off to me. She wants a picture for her mama
in Shanghai who, wearing coveralls, paints yellow hair on novelty angels for America.

When I sleep, I see vixen eyes that leap like sparklers into ditches. I see pleather bears
searching for honey in the marigolds that find themselves encased in amber waves
    of dew.

Do I think every dream should be a dream that someone has of you, America?

IN THE WOMEN'S HOSPITAL

—Chengdu, Sichuan

Let Zhu Kui guide me through thickets of women to the frosting-pink exam
    room door.

Let the masked technician wave us in.

Let a woman, pantsless on a table, chat with one of twenty more waiting in the
    open room.

Let them joke, clean their nails, pass sunflower seeds without looking the way
    lovers or sisters do.

Let Zhu Kui demand, in the name of my Americanness, a privacy screen.

Let the tech, her mask ballooning with exhalation, push the screen in.

Let Zhu Kui nudge me toward a table, its sanitary paper dark with wetness.

Let me imagine the wet spot smells of daisies, blood, and lime.

Let the tech lay a blue paper square on the wet spot.

Let me pull my jeans and underwear down, let them dangle from my right foot.

Let Zhu Kui shoo ogling women behind the screen.

Let me position my butt on the paper square.

Let the tech wave her ultrasound wand.

Let Zhu Kui shoo the women back again.

Let the tech gesture toward the computer screen: my ovary, dark with life.

Let someone behind the curtain say a word I understand: Mandarin for "open."

Let me feel all that *kaifang*, applied to U.S. women, insinuates.

Let me recall watching Rose say, *put your hands on me, Jack*, in a sold-out Chengdu
    theater.

Let me understand another word, the one for *foreigner*.

Let me remember phone cameras clicking at me on the subway.

Let me relive an argument: I called *laowai* an ugly word, and Eric said the virtue
    of a noun is truth, the virtue of truth neutrality.

Let dust motes, like stars or stones, rise toward the sky impartially.

Let me remember arriving in Chengdu, where traffic zinged like neutrons with no
    nucleus, asking Xiaoping if China had traffic cops, and *just because you haven't*
    seen the iridescent center of a thing doesn't mean it has no heart is what he said,
    but the words he used were *look, there's one.*

Let me think *kaifang open laowai foreigner.*

Let me see four hearts of light rising.

Let a woman lean around the privacy curtain.

Let me, before Zhu Kui whisks her back, look between my stirrupped feet into
    the woman's eyes.
Let us each know ourselves as wild, spinning universes.
Let us each feel tethered to a single center, dizzy.

WHEN I WRITE *HEART* I MEAN

to write *hearth*, but the chalk breaks off.
My students draw a line from *heart* down to my illustration of a chimneyed fire
and say that, in America, the hearts are bright.
They flicker. If you edge too close, welts rise like diamonds on your arms.

speech speec

I go to a restaurant with Sunny and Carly, who've taken English names.
I try to say, in Mandarin, that I like ribs, but I say *pi* instead of *pai*, which means
I've told them I like eating sweet-and-sour butts.
They say I'm like a light-eyed panda padding across town: rare, incomprehensible.

marsh Mars

The waiter brings us ribs, and I recall the youthful Middle Eastern man
who, pre-lunch at my brother's bar—The Swamp—offered his resident alien card
    for ID.
None of us knew how to say his name. I never took the time to ask.
We called him *E.T.* behind his back until the day he moved away.

booth boot

I ask Sunny and Carly where I can go to learn kung fu. I say *Bruce Lee, Jet Li, Donnie
    Yen*.
They laugh, talk low together, lead me to the movie ticket booth.
Afterwards they say that kung fu is for kids and elder men.
They call me *Gongfu Yeye*, laughing. They say, *kick me, kick me, kung fu grandfather*.

cloth clot

My shoes are too impractical and, walking home, blood leaks through my sole.
Sunny takes me to her family's house. Her mom is watching game shows on her
    iPhone.
She props it against a peach and keeps her eyes on it as she cups my heel
in her bare palm, pours water, smooths salve like laundered sheets.
The gauze she fastens catches blood the way a hearth hangs onto heat.

ELEGY WITH LAKE EFFECT

A blizzard switched the ground
for clouds and made the county blind
the day you climbed into the tub

and dropped to quell the rising
pressure of your body. I move by touch
through the blank meadow of heaven.

Here's the front path of roof-ice
crashing, the sidewalk of what's
underneath and splits: fish knife,

glass pipe, painted angel dolls,
rope of firecracker shells.
Are you that spill of paperbacks,

spines cracked, in puddle-ice?
Are you wind that stiffens leggings
on the line and doesn't give

a damn that my gutters wail
and rip loose from their eaves?
Then I don't give a damn either.

When I tear my shirt, when I
chop my braids off at the nape,
I'm only stockpiling beds

for summer's goslings. When I
kneel in the snow and scream,
I'm chiseling all the lost books free

by striking breath on bone.

IN FAVOR OF DEFENESTRATION

Flapping broke the Peng bird's wing,
But its wind will stir the world forever.

—Li Bai's final poem, "Death Song"

Maybe I should let feathers fall
as they'll fly: On the moon, like stone;
in water, swaying, reflected as they drown,
Li Bai–like—by which I mean drunk,
in love with the moon of the river. Line up
for ledge-stands, children, books open.
This lesson concerns whether stones
can grow wings. First, a chapter on Li Bai
who lost his wings. He tied two fans
scapula-high and tried to woo the moon
while her face rested on the Yangtze.
The lesson says his robes flamingoed
skyward—a reflection, I once thought,
of flight. But please see figure 4,
which shows that he crashed, hands first,
like a drunk into cake. Of course, by *a drunk,*
I mean *the Peng bird,* and *cake* means *the wings*
of his last river. Children, before we jump in,
consider the ghost of the moon
in water's mirror. Some say it's a reflection
of heaven—others say it's flying stone.
The lesson here: Teachers lie,
so field-test all lessons. If the moon calls,
say maybe. I mean, get drunk on glue fumes;
bend whalebone; tie springs.
Reflect: How best to climb the wind?
Kids, we must make wings. They say
Mount Tangula rises moonward like
balloons do, but that's a metaphor. It erodes
daily, dwindling before the Yangtze,
where waves recite the lessons of people

who flew like hunted ducks into the moon's
pale image. I mean, they jumped. Some
were drunk. Let's remember: Not all
who leap discover they have wings, but some
manage to dance on down, reflected
in the river's blue, which is sky reflecting
over riverbed. I feel like a pebble yearning
for currents to launch me high, but stones
don't gain wings by wishing,
my featherless sons and daughters. Close
the books. Once we've drunk deep
of open air, we'll step as onto moon-face
reflected in water. Lessons alone can't fortify us,
my fellow stones, so the drunker, the better.
I mean, may wings swim us to the moon.

LAKE ASTRONOMY

On every star, I wished for flight
but, in Superior, I feared it.
My feet scrambled
for her stony floor, but Kelly
—air-boned, limbs fluent
as skipping rocks—soared in.
Our teacher said Laika the dog
flew into space and flies there still,
a star, but I knew that stars
are gas burning with particles,
and dogs are dogs that roast
or drown, pinned down
by airlessness. My cousin
bobbed and dove and, when
Superior's arm struck coast,
she vanished. I toe-counted
one pebble for each intrepid kid
and mongrel lost, unsleeping,
in the lake's roiling galaxy. But look:
Suddenly, Kelly jettisoned herself free:
She growled bright past the stars.

LETTER TO MY TEENAGED SELF: YOU ARE A HOUSE, YOU ARE A HAMMER, YOU'RE THE MOMENTUM OF THE NAIL

In many ways you'll always pull on boots
to rise from bed and walk from room to room
and hear the jagged gypsum moan beneath
your rubber heel and love the girl
in eyeliner and duct-taped shoes
(how casually she shrugs while kicking holes
in walls and car windows) or love at least
the way a single winter break with her
(your parents think you're off with church-
group friends) lets you discover what an art
destruction is so rip the flocked bucolics
from their glue rejoice because your limestone-
powdered biceps are the pulleys
of the sledgehammer that is the lever
of the fall and scrutinize the cat
who rides the pendulum of gravity
from bandsaw down to baseboard
for she crashes like a nail advancing
through a tunnel of its own design
so when you raise the scaffold of your limbs
(four limbs two torsos O) be long and long
for salt that rises through the skin and hail
each thing that splintered (paper drywall oak)
yes hail the tool belt for the way it grips
and then descends your open pelvic cage
and hail the ceiling of your skull
the thumping of your mitral floor
remember that tomorrow dawn
will enter like a woman fallen
on this floor in broken gypsum budding
she will cleave nighttime and day the way
a sledgehammer cleaves wood and wood the way
a week will cleave a girl and her next self
or breeze will cleave to flesh that is the wall
of this the house the nail the body.

WHEN I SAY *THUMPING MITRAL FLOOR* I MEAN

that if you want to know where lightning strikes   inhale

and count the beats that pass before your walls begin to shake

when I was young   I screamed at thunderstorms

my mother rubbed my heaving chest while whispering

breathe deep   breathe deep   breathe deep

HEROIC ORIGIN

I forget it's not the buzz that hunts me

bush to steps to bolted door forget the buzz

isn't the sting that burns isn't the lump

or plunge of EpiPen isn't the autumn mound

of gloss-winged dead forget that first was layered wax

and mud-round house the queen and drones

the gold congealed and chambered up forget

that kids stand still to save themselves hair rising at the root while

grandma-eyes rise eave to hive that shakes

when grandpa hits the wall or swings a kitten by

its broken tail forget the buzz of worker bees

functions to shake the pollen loose to build the hive

as grandma sweeps the porch remembering

fistfuls of dewed cloudberry blooms shined shoes

that wink she knows a hive's a packed-in queen

a thousand kids that dip their heads and rile their legs

remember Saara when the buzzing hones on you

that those who pitched this welting fire also filled chamber

after chamber chamber chamber with a humming wall of gold

SELFIE AS WHAT BREAKS

What I've forgotten of compromise
I know of sacrifice: the spent
myocardium. The faith that makes
men tear temples down. There's a boy:
his voice. A woman: the tide that
sweeps her baby in. Frogs into
song. Thunderstorm and then elm. Me:
bridge. Me: milk tooth. Me: awl of dawn
that perforates horizon's belt.

They demand splint and plaster, nail
and brace and glue. They beg grass to bend
for a meadow of runners, but a pliable wish
will die inside the bone.

To get a hundred million parts,
you must ransom one whole.
Just pray fingernail, levee, fever.
I promise to wait for you where
the high-tensile fence divides intact
from fracture, but I'm also cross-knuckled
fingers that say *undo, undo.*

IN THE ABSENCE OF SPARROWS, I LEARNED TO STOP HEARING SPARROWS

once, drunk, I tripped into the fire and saw
sparks spitting off my boots and howled, *hey, I
invented stars*, and Kelly laughed until she peed,
and yelled, *in outer space, stars are just flying dirt*.
she meant that if you spend your life awakening
only to sparrow song, you'll mistake
whatever noise surprises you for the defensive call
of small brown birds from North America.

so for a year in Guizhou, I only heard sparrows.
at breakfast, when I retched, complained
my pastry had a hot dog hidden inside
they sang   when I refused to taste *chou dofu*
they sang   when I used Miao batik to dry my shoes
they sang   when I hugged Zhu Kui without asking
they sang   when she pulled away and stuttered like crushed fire
they sang   but wait—she stuttered like crushed fire
they stung   but wait: she stuttered. like crushed fire.
they rang like a hoop struck by a basketball. I swallowed
pickled breakfast egg, and sparrows warbled
like forged iPhones. I read up on farmers beating pots
and waving sticks against the sparrowed sky, and sparrows
blared like car horns. I read how trucks would overflow
with blood-feathered, shattered wings, and sparrow-
shush began to sound like women sweeping streets. I opened
my window and heard sparrowsong—no—I heard
jackhammers rat-a-tat the mountain down.

I listened as Zhu Kui said that since the pest campaign,
you hardly saw a sparrow there, and a bike wheel whined unlike
a sparrow sings. when she offered to French-braid my hair
and I said, *s'il vous plait*, her laugh sounded nothing like
a sparrow sings. We clambered up the mountain's
exposed flank, lit fireworks and laughed, and I whispered
to Zhu Kui that stars were fire that I would never
touch, and finally I could hear nothing singing.

HAPPILY EVER AFTER

once upon a time the forest opened like an atrium

to pull us in   we drizzled through

snow brambles   into marsh   and in the marsh

there was a sugared house   that when it saw

the wolf of us   unlocked itself   and once upon

a time   the witch's heart   (which was a heart

inside a heart   that beat inside

the homeland's chest)   applauded us

she fed us lime and frankincense   and once upon

someone had left   a trail of stones   like stars

to guide us back   after we'd killed the witch

the way you clear-cut   and tidy any unpaved thing

once upon   her heart clapped time and   dying

closed upon itself   the witch is dead in brain

but since her heart knocks on   we keep her up

with plungers in the vein   machines that beep

our medicine is thumbs   and fingertips

but once upon   a doctor would use her ear

to find the part   that never sleeps   the blood

and chambered meat   that's like a rock squeezed

in a fist   rapping its knuckles

on the sweet door   of the body.

WHENEVER I SAY *HEART* I MEAN

that even with no hand or face or stomach left

the Lion Heart   like someone grand and perfect

in her hunger   kept on breathing breathing breathing

so see that girl as light   see heart-chambers of light that rise

and fall in lead-dark hospital   imagine

bedsheets filled   and flattened   filled

ACKNOWLEDGMENTS

The writing of this manuscript was made possible in part by a grant from the Southwest Minnesota Arts Council with funds appropriated by the McKnight Foundation.

Thank you to the editors of the journals, anthologies, and chapbooks in which these poems appeared or will appear, sometimes under other titles or in slightly different forms.

Best of the Net 2016 (anthology published by Sundress Publications): "Letter to My Teenaged Self: You Are a House, You Are a Hammer, You're the Momentum of the Nail"

Birmingham Poetry Review: "Heroic Origin"

Blackbird: "Elegy with Lake Effect"

cream city review: "In the Absence of Sparrows, I Learn to Stop Hearing Sparrows," "When I write *heart* I mean"

Eureka Literary Magazine: "Lake Astronomy," "Once upon America"

Here: Women Writing on Michigan's Upper Peninsula (anthology published by Michigan State University Press, 2015): "All I know of white"

Iron Horse Literary Review: "Canticle for Waitresses, Waiting"

Linebreak: "The wolf in the trailer,"

Milk Tooth, Levee, Fever (chapbook published by Dancing Girl Press): "All I know of white," "Spawning Season," "Selfie as What Breaks," "Torch"

Nine Mile Magazine: "Little Red and Little Red," "Paradise by the Paulding Light," "Superman and Batman Sleep Over"

[PANK]: "In Favor of Defenestration"

Pith: "Heart of Lion, Heart of Light"

Radar: "Selfie as Elly the Doll"

A Story of America Goes Walking (art chapbook published by Shechem Press): "Happily Ever After," "Heart of Lion, Heart of Light," "In the Women's Hospital," "Once upon America," "Psalm with Pleather Teddy Bears," "The wolf in the trailer,"

Subtropics: "Winter Correspondence"

32 Poems: "All I know of white"

Tinderbox Poetry Journal: "Psalm with Pleather Teddy Bears," "Selfie as What Breaks"

Up the Staircase: "Spawning Season"

Valparaiso Poetry Review: "Torch"

Vinyl Poetry and Prose: "Letter to My Teenaged Self: You Are a House, You Are a Hammer, You're the Momentum of the Nail"

JUNIPER
JUNIPER PRIZE FOR POETRY

This volume is the fifty-third recipient of the
Juniper Prize for Poetry, established in 1975 by
University of Massachusetts Press in collaboration with
the UMass Amherst MFA program for Poets and Writers.
The prize is named in honor of the poet Robert Francis
(1901–1987), who for many years lived in Fort Juniper,
a tiny home of his own construction, in Amherst.

ANN HAZELWOOD

CHRISTMAS,

She Wrote

50+ Heartwarming
Short Stories, Tidbits & More

C&T PUBLISHING
Another Maker Inspired!